There are Stranger Stars

by

W.B. Clark

There are Stranger Stars

ISBN: 979-8-9865649-1-3

Copyright © 2023 by W.B. Clark

All rights reserved.

www.wbclarkbooks.com

For all the adults who still dream of Magic

There are stranger stars out there

go find them

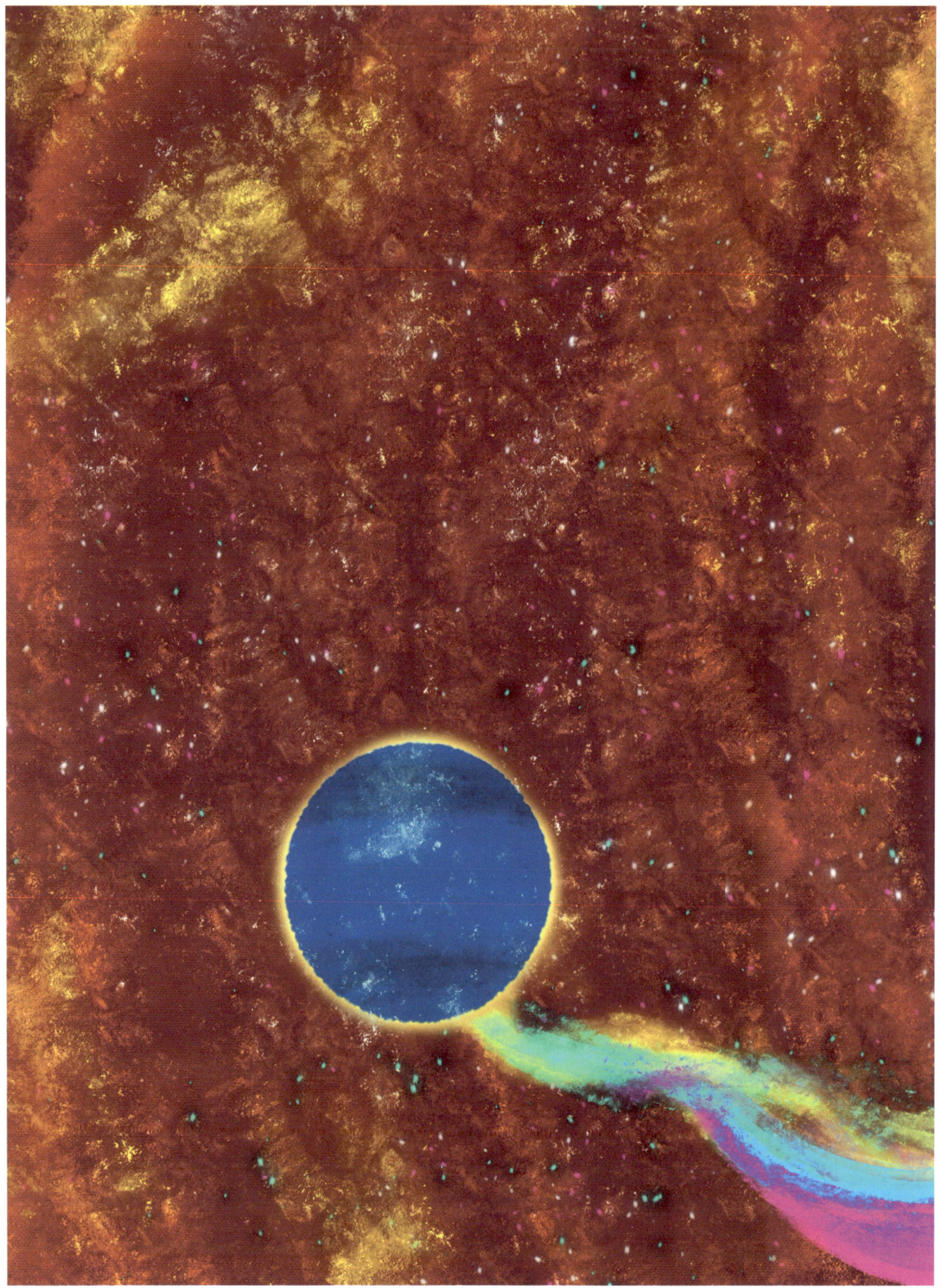

The light can shine brilliantly
Yet darkness can still creep in
You can have everything in the universe
and still feel sorrow
Nonetheless
You are a beacon
So even if your base is cracked
and your soul weary
take a rest
then stand again

Sometimes an *angry* heart just needs to borrow from a kind one

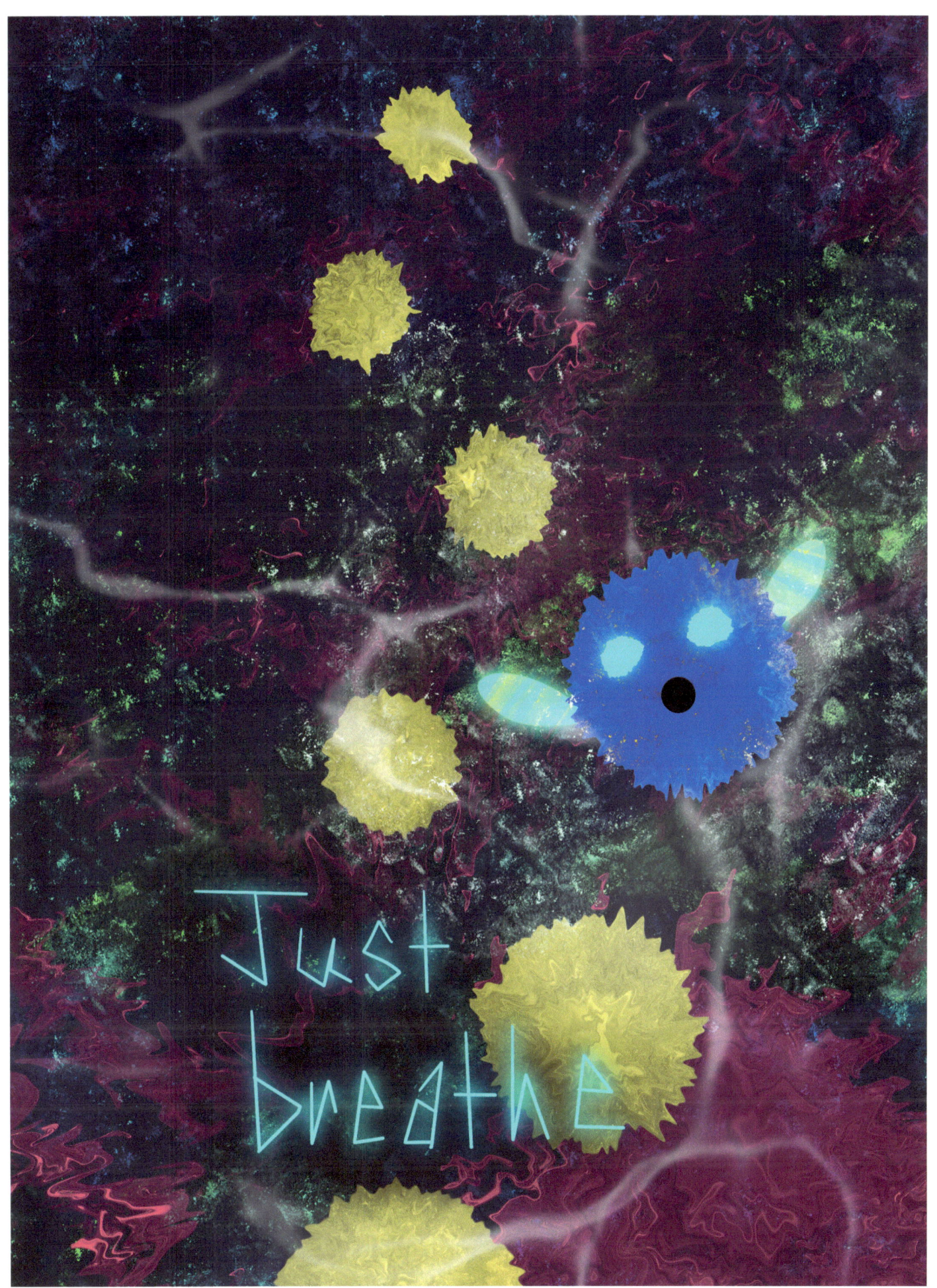

I get to be right here

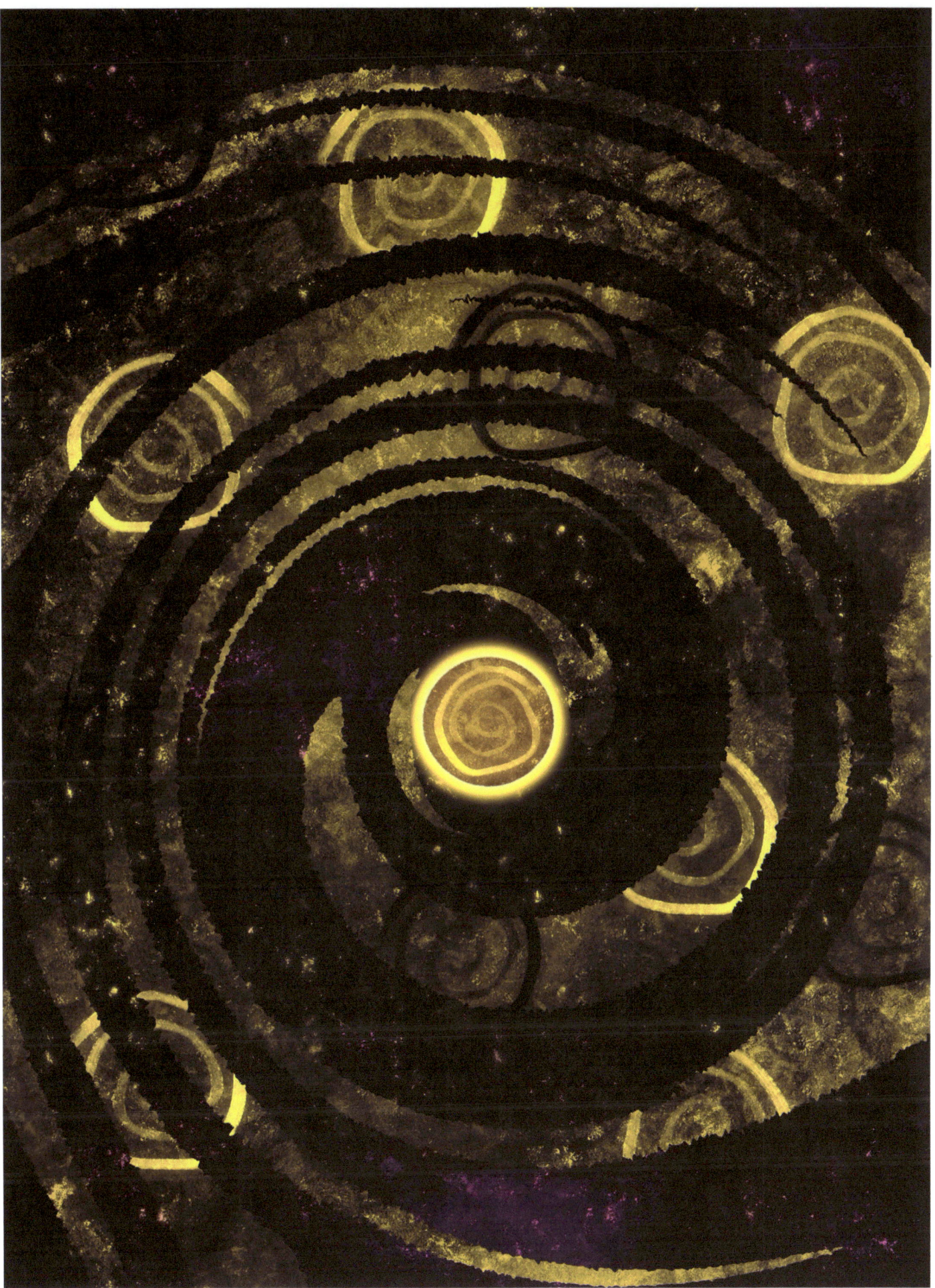

Found You

Thank you for reading!

For additional books & art by W.B. Clark,

visit: www.wbclarkbooks.com

Adult Titles:

A Thousand Short Lives

Future Adult Titles:

Giving Up Elysium

Heart of Áïdes

For Children:

So You Want to Be a Witch?

ABOUT THE AUTHOR

W.B. Clark is from small-town Oklahoma, mostly raised on a farm full of chickens and then partially on a boat in Alaska. She graduated from the University of Oklahoma, then moved to some big cities, where life happened. She finally got a job that pays her bills, and sometimes, she gets to write books and illustrate pretty pictures on the side. In between, she plays random instruments poorly, swears often, and wonders where her next adventure will be. Some of which involve hiking, camping, scuba diving, and starting complex projects she knows little to nothing about. She loves breakfast, good friends, and hearing other people's stories.

www.ingramcontent.com/pod-product-compliance
Lightning Source LLC
Chambersburg PA
CBHW041423010526
44119CB00015B/356